Table of Content

Table of Content 1
Chapter 1: Introduction 2
Chapter 2: Oskar Schindler's Childhood 8
Chapter 3: Schindler's Rise to Power 17
Chapter 4: The Nazi Occupation 25
Chapter 5: Schindler's List 32
Chapter 6: Life in the Krakow Ghetto 39
Chapter 7: Plaszow Labor Camp 47
Chapter 8: The Escape 55
Chapter 9: Schindler's Legacy 62
Chapter 10: Conclusion 69

CHAPTER 1: INTRODUCTION

A brief history of the Holocaust

While the gravity of this topic demands a sensitive approach, it is important to convey these facts with a professional and academic tone that remains approachable and friendly to ensure a deeper understanding of this tragic one in mankind's history.

Historical Context:
To fully comprehend the Holocaust, it is essential to understand the historical circumstances that gave rise to such abominable acts. Anti-Semitism, the centuries-old hatred and discrimination against Jews, had persisted throughout Europe for centuries. In Germany, the stage was set for the Holocaust in the aftermath of World War I when the country faced economic upheaval and political instability. Adolf Hitler rose to power in 1933, promoting a fascist ideology that aimed to create a racially superior society, with Jews being scapegoated as the root of all problems. The Nazis skillfully utilized propaganda, indoctrination, and repression to secure their hold on power and set the Holocaust into motion.

Nazi Persecution:
Under Hitler's leadership, the Nazis implemented a

systematic campaign of persecution against Jews, aiming to isolate, dehumanize, and ultimately annihilate them. The Nuremberg Laws of 1935 stripped German Jews of their citizenship and basic rights, separating them from the rest of society. Jewish-owned businesses were boycotted, and Jews were excluded from universities and professions. As the Nazis expanded their influence across Europe with the outbreak of war, their persecution extended to other countries with the goal of establishing a "Final Solution" - the complete extermination of the Jewish people.

The Ghettos and Concentration Camps:
To further isolate and control Jews, the Nazis enforced the establishment of ghettos in occupied territories. These were often cramped, overcrowded quarters where Jews lived in abject poverty and squalor, segregated from the rest of society. The ghettos served as temporary holding areas before planned mass deportations to extermination camps, where systematic killing on an industrial scale occurred. Auschwitz, Treblinka, and Sobibor are among the infamous extermination camps where millions of innocent lives were mercilessly extinguished through gas chambers, mass shootings, and forced labor.

Resistance and Rescue:
Despite the overwhelming odds, there were courageous acts of resistance against the Nazis both inside and outside the ghettos and camps. Jewish partisans, such as the Bielski brothers in Belarus, organized armed resistance against the Nazis, saving countless lives. Additionally, non-Jewish individuals and organizations risked their lives to hide Jewish families or facilitate their escape, known as the "Righteous Among the Nations." These acts of bravery highlight the resilience and determination of those who fought against the Nazi regime and their genocidal policies.

Liberation and Aftermath:
As Allied forces began to liberate territories occupied by the Nazis, the true horror of the Holocaust was exposed. Soldiers, journalists, and local populations came face to face with emaciated survivors, mass graves, and evidence of the systematic destruction. The Nuremberg Trials, held after the war, sought to hold Nazi leaders accountable for their crimes against humanity. The magnitude of the Holocaust forever changed the perception of genocide and played a pivotal role in the creation of the Universal Declaration of Human Rights by the United Nations in 1948.

The Holocaust remains an indelible scar on human history, serving as a reminder of humanity's capacity for evil, hatred, and discrimination. It is crucial not only to remember the victims but also to learn from this dark one to prevent such atrocities from recurring. By studying and understanding the Holocaust with a professional and approachable tone, we can honor the victims, pay tribute to the survivors, and work collectively towards fostering a more inclusive and tolerant world.

Introduction to Oskar Schindler

Oskar Schindler, a German industrialist and member of the Nazi Party, is a figure who defies easy categorization. Though initially motivated by personal gain and political expedience, Schindler's remarkable transformation from opportunist to righteous rescuer has earned him a place in history as a revered hero. His story, immortalized in Steven Spielberg's 1993 film "Schindler's List," serves as a testament to the power of individual actions and the potential for redemption in even the darkest times.

Born on April 28, 1908, in the industrial city of Zwittau, Moravia, which was then part of the Austro-Hungarian Empire, Oskar Schindler grew up in a world on the brink of change. As a young man, he showed an early aptitude for business and entrepreneurship, embarking on ventures that would pave the way for his later success. After studying engineering and economics at the University of Prague, he ventured into the world of commerce, taking his first steps on the path that would eventually intersect with history.

Amidst the rise of the Nazi Party and Adolf Hitler's ascent to power in Germany, Schindler's ambition and opportunism led him to join the party in 1939. At that time, aligning oneself with the Nazi regime seemed a pragmatic move, promising access to resources and economic advantages. As a member of the party, Schindler secured contracts and connections that would prove critical in the years to come.

In 1939, Schindler's fortunes took a significant turn when he purchased an enamelware factory in Krakow, Poland, initially known as Deutsche Emaillewaren-Fabrik, or DEF. This factory would become the setting for Schindler's extraordinary acts of bravery and humanity, providing him with both a stage and the means to save the lives of over 1,200 Jewish individuals during the Holocaust.

Despite the dominant anti-Semitic ideology propagated by the Nazi regime, Schindler's interactions with Jewish workers at his factory awakened a sense of empathy and compassion. Witnessing firsthand the horrifying conditions imposed upon them by the Nazis, he experienced a profound change of heart. Recognizing the profound injustice and suffering inflicted upon the Jewish population, Schindler embarked on a mission to intervene and create opportunities for survival.

Utilizing his wealth, connections, and cunning, Schindler employed Jewish workers in his factory, effectively shielding them from deportation to concentration camps. He became known for his ability to negotiate with the German authorities, convincing them that the Jewish labor force was indispensable to the wartime economy. This allowed him to protect his workers, providing them with food, shelter, and safety within the confines of his factory walls.

Schindler's List, a document containing the names of the Jewish individuals he saved, is a testament to his determination and audacity. By surreptitiously including the names of individuals who had not been employed in his factory, Schindler secured their survival through his sheer willpower and tenacity. This extraordinary feat was achieved at great personal risk, as Schindler constantly navigated the treacherous and shifting politics of Nazi-occupied Poland.

In 1944, as the Nazis sought to liquidate the Krakow ghetto and deport its inhabitants to the Auschwitz concentration camp, Schindler intervened once again. Through bribery, he persuaded the SS guards to allow his workers to be transported to a sub-camp in what is now the Czech Republic. This relocation ultimately saved them from certain death, as Allied forces were closing in on both Auschwitz and the impending collapse of the Third Reich.

Following the end of World War II in 1945, Oskar Schindler faced an uncertain future. He was penniless and burdened with the weight of his actions during the war. However, his selfless efforts did not go unnoticed, and the Jewish survivors he had saved held him in deep reverence and gratitude. Many of them went on to testify about his heroism, sharing their stories of survival and the indelible impact Schindler had made on their lives.

Schindler's transformation from Nazi party member to righteous rescuer serves as a powerful example of the potential for individuals to confront and challenge the prevailing social and political norms of their time. His actions during the Holocaust have inspired countless others to stand up against injustice and oppression, reinforcing the belief that even in the darkest of times, there is always hope. Starting as a member of the Nazi Party motivated by personal gain, Schindler's encounters with the suffering of Jewish individuals under Nazi rule changed him profoundly. By utilizing his position as a factory owner, he saved the lives of more than 1,200 Jews, defying the prevailing ideology and risking his own safety. Schindler's actions during the Holocaust offer hope and inspiration, reminding us of the potential for individuals to rise above the circumstances and impact the world for the better. His legacy serves as a timeless reminder of the power of compassion, empathy, and the capacity for redemption.

CHAPTER 2: OSKAR SCHINDLER'S CHILDHOOD

Early life and upbringing

The early years of a person's life are marked by rapid physical, cognitive, and emotional changes. It is during this time that the brain undergoes significant development and establishes neural pathways that will influence the individual throughout their lifespan. From birth to around five years of age, children experience immense growth in their motor skills, language development, and social interactions. It is a crucial period characterized by curiosity, exploration, and tremendous learning potential.

Parents, caregivers, and immediate surroundings play a pivotal role in shaping a child's early life experiences. The quality of these interactions greatly influences a child's emotional and social development. Nurturing and responsive care fosters secure attachment, which provides a foundation for healthy relationships and emotional well-being. Conversely, neglectful or abusive environments can have detrimental effects on a child's overall development, leading to long-term emotional and behavioral challenges.

Cultural and socioeconomic factors also significantly impact a child's early life and upbringing. Different cultures have unique practices, beliefs, and values that shape a child's worldview and socialization. Economic circumstances can affect access to quality education, healthcare, and social opportunities, ultimately influencing a child's future prospects. Recognizing and understanding these contextual factors is crucial in accurately comprehending the influences on an individual's early life experiences.

Education and early childhood interventions play a crucial role in supporting positive development during the early years. High-quality early education programs have been shown to enhance cognitive abilities, promote social skills, and improve academic performance. Early interventions, such as parent education and support programs, are also effective in providing families with the knowledge and resources needed to create nurturing environments for their children. By investing in early childhood education and interventions, societies can ensure that all children have equal opportunities for success and well-being.

The impact of early life and upbringing extends beyond childhood and continues to shape individuals into adulthood. Early experiences form the building blocks of one's personality and significantly influence their attitudes, values, and beliefs. The attachment style established during infancy can affect the way individuals form relationships throughout their lives. A secure attachment fosters trust, empathy, and resilience, while an insecure attachment can result in difficulties forming and maintaining healthy relationships.

Early life experiences also influence cognitive development, including problem-solving skills, memory, and critical thinking abilities. Children who receive stimulating and enriching environments tend to have higher cognitive abilities than those who grow up in impoverished or neglectful settings. Furthermore, early exposure to language and literacy-rich environments promotes strong literacy skills, setting the stage for academic success later in life.

The impact of early life and upbringing extends beyond individual development and has broader implications for society as a whole. Research consistently shows that investing in early childhood development yields significant long-term benefits. Individuals who receive quality early education and support are more likely to finish school, obtain higher-paying jobs, and contribute positively to their communities. Moreover, early interventions focused on vulnerable populations can help break intergenerational cycles of poverty and inequality. The experiences, interactions, and environments children encounter during the formative years shape their physical, cognitive, and emotional well-being. Acknowledging and understanding the impact of early life experiences is crucial for creating supportive environments and implementing effective early childhood interventions. By prioritizing investments in early childhood development, societies can foster a generation of individuals who are equipped with the skills, resilience, and opportunities for a brighter future.

Influences that shaped his worldview

The formation of an individual's worldview is an intricate and multifaceted process that involves numerous factors. In the case of the person we are discussing, understanding the influences that have contributed to shaping his worldview is essential to gaining deeper insight into his perspectives and beliefs. This exploration will delve into the various external forces that have played pivotal roles in his intellectual development. By examining these influences, we can decipher the origins of his ideas, values, and principles, and gain a clearer understanding of his unique perspective on the world.

One of the most significant influences on his worldview comes from his family background. Growing up in a household that deeply valued education and critical thinking, he was exposed to a vast array of intellectual discussions from a young age. His parents, both intellectuals themselves, fostered an environment of curiosity, encouraging him to question, challenge, and explore ideas. This nurturing environment allowed him to develop a strong appetite for knowledge and a deep appreciation for the power of ideas. By being raised in this intellectually stimulating environment, he developed a lifelong passion for learning and the pursuit of truth, which profoundly shaped his worldview.

Education undoubtedly played a pivotal role in shaping his views. A formal education can expose individuals to diverse perspectives, impart critical thinking skills, and encourage intellectual discourse. In his case, he was fortunate to attend institutions that prioritized an interdisciplinary approach, placing equal emphasis on the sciences, humanities, and social sciences. This comprehensive education equipped him with a broad base of knowledge that allowed him to see the interconnectedness of different fields of study. By exploring various disciplines, he developed a holistic understanding of the world, honed his analytical abilities, and learned how to effectively navigate complex topics. This diverse educational experience significantly influenced the formation of his worldview.

Mentorship has also emerged as a crucial influence on his intellectual development. Throughout his journey, he had the privilege of working with accomplished individuals who guided, challenged, and inspired him. These mentors offered valuable insights, exposed him to new ideas, and provided constructive feedback to help refine his thought processes. Their guidance played a vital role in shaping his worldview by broadening his perspectives, challenging his assumptions, and helping him cultivate a more nuanced understanding of the world. The mentorship he received helped him hone his critical thinking skills, articulate his thoughts concisely, and approach complex issues with open-mindedness. The impact of these mentoring relationships is indelible in his intellectual journey.

Beyond these personal influences, wider societal factors also shaped his worldview. The socio-political climate in which he grew up cannot be overlooked when discussing the influences that shaped his perspectives. The cultural, economic, and political factors prevailing in his formative years had a profound impact on his worldview. The events and social movements that unfolded during his youth shaped his understanding of justice, equality, and human rights. Experiencing societal changes, witnessing moments of upheaval, and observing both progress and setbacks influenced his beliefs and values. These broader societal influences, layered upon his personal experiences, contributed to the unique tapestry of his worldview.

The influence of literature and the arts cannot be underestimated either. Engaging with literature, whether it be non-fiction, novels, or poetry, enriched his imagination, expanded his empathetic capabilities, and deepened his understanding of the human condition. Artistic expressions, from visual arts to music and theater, allowed him to engage with diverse perspectives, explore emotions, and connect with the larger human experience. These aesthetic encounters challenged his preconceived notions, broadened his horizons, and ultimately influenced his worldview by fostering a deep appreciation for the power of human creativity and expression.

Lastly, it is essential to acknowledge the impact of personal experiences on shaping his worldview. Traveling, meeting people from different cultures and backgrounds, and encountering firsthand the richness of diversity have undoubtedly played a significant role in his intellectual development. Immersion in different environments and exposure to various perspectives have allowed him to challenge his own biases, recognize the commonalities among individuals, and gain a more nuanced understanding of the world. These explorations and experiences have shaped his worldview by fostering a sense of empathy, curiosity, and interconnectedness among all human beings. His family upbringing, educational experiences, mentorship relationships, societal context, encounters with literature and the arts, and personal experiences have all played pivotal roles in shaping his perspectives, beliefs, and values. By closely examining these influences, we gain valuable insights into the foundation of his worldview. Understanding the interplay between these different factors allows us to appreciate the complexity of his intellectual journey and the richness of his perspectives.

Impact of early experiences on his future actions

It is widely acknowledged that our early experiences play a crucial role in shaping our attitudes, beliefs, and behaviors later in life. This concept is often attributed to the theory of developmental stages put forth by renowned psychologist Erik Erikson, who asserted that our early childhood experiences greatly influence our ability to navigate social interactions and establish a strong sense of identity. In this one, we will explore how specific early experiences can shape an individual's future actions and how understanding this interplay can contribute to personal growth and development.

1. The Power of Attachment:

One of the most influential early experiences that can shape an individual's future actions is the quality of their attachment to primary caregivers. Attachment theory, developed by John Bowlby, posits that the nature of the parent-child bond established during infancy sets the foundation for relationships and emotional regulation throughout life. Infants who experience secure attachment, characterized by consistent and responsive care, tend to develop a sense of trust and confidence in their relationships. This early sense of security influences their future actions, making them more likely to engage in healthy relationships and exhibit prosocial behavior. On the other hand, insecure attachment, resulting from inconsistent or neglectful care, can lead to difficulties in forming meaningful connections and can manifest in maladaptive behaviors like aggression or withdrawal.

2. Impact of Parenting Styles:

The parenting style employed by caregivers can also have a profound impact on an individual's future actions. Research suggests that parenting styles fall on a continuum ranging from authoritarian to permissive, with authoritative parenting being the ideal middle ground. Authoritative parents provide a balance of warmth and discipline, encouraging independence while setting clear expectations. Children raised by authoritative parents often develop positive self-regulation skills and display greater emotional intelligence. These early experiences foster a sense of autonomy and self-efficacy, shaping future actions that are confident, responsible, and considerate of others. Conversely, authoritarian or permissive parenting can result in future actions characterized by a lack of self-control, defiance, or an inability to handle challenges effectively.

3. Influence of Early Peer Interactions:

Beyond the family environment, early interactions with peers can significantly impact an individual's future actions. During childhood and adolescence, peer relationships become increasingly influential in shaping behavior. Positive experiences with peers, such as forming friendships and engaging in prosocial activities, can foster social skills, empathy, and cooperation. These early positive interactions lay the groundwork for future actions that promote healthy relationships, teamwork, and collaboration. However, negative peer experiences, such as bullying or social exclusion, can lead to the development of maladaptive coping strategies or a propensity for aggressive behavior. Recognizing and addressing such negative experiences is therefore crucial to promoting positive future actions.

4. Early Experiences and Cognitive Development:

Cognitive development is another important aspect influenced by early experiences, which subsequently shapes an individual's future actions. Early experiences that stimulate intellectual growth and provide opportunities for exploration and learning play a pivotal role in fostering cognitive development. A stimulating and responsive environment promotes curiosity, creativity, and problem-solving skills, setting the stage for future actions driven by an eagerness to learn and adapt. Conversely, deprived or neglectful environments can hinder cognitive development, resulting in future actions that may be marked by reduced academic achievement, diminished problem-solving abilities, and limited educational and vocational opportunities.

5. Adverse Childhood Experiences (ACEs) and Future Actions:

Adverse Childhood Experiences (ACEs), such as abuse, neglect, or household dysfunction, can profoundly impact an individual's future actions. A landmark study by Felitti et al. (1998) highlighted the long-term consequences of ACEs, indicating a strong correlation between childhood adversity and negative adult outcomes, including physical and mental health issues, substance abuse, and involvement in criminal activities. Such experiences during the early years may lead individuals to develop maladaptive coping strategies or engage in risky behaviors as a means of dealing with the trauma experienced. Recognizing the potential impact of ACEs is essential, as it informs the development of prevention and intervention strategies that aim to mitigate the long-term consequences and promote positive future actions.

Early experiences undeniably shape an individual's future actions. From attachment relationships to parenting styles, peer interactions, cognitive development, and exposure to adversity, every aspect of a person's early life can influence their beliefs, attitudes, and behaviors in later years. Understanding this interplay is crucial for professionals working with individuals across various domains, including education, mental health, and social services. By recognizing the impact of early experiences, we can provide the necessary support and interventions to foster resilience, emotional well-being, and positive future actions, ultimately contributing to personal growth and overall societal welfare.

CHAPTER 3: SCHINDLER'S RISE TO POWER

Schindler's business ventures

Schindler's entry into the enamelware business stemmed from a desire to exploit the opportunities presented during the war. In 1939, he purchased a bankrupt factory previously owned by the Judenrat, a Jewish council that was forcibly established by the occupying Nazi regime. Renovating the factory and renaming it "Deutsche Emailwarenfabrik," Schindler began producing enamel kitchenware, benefiting from the deprived labor market resulting from the mass eviction and extermination of Jewish populations. By employing Jewish workers who had been deemed "essential" by the Germans, Schindler secured an inexpensive and easily exploitable workforce while catering to the acute demand for enamel goods.

The success of Schindler's enamelware factory allowed him to expand his business interests, and he soon established his own trading company. Through his unrestricted access to goods and materials, he profited significantly in the black market. This trading business provided him with valuable connections and an opportunity to build relationships with influential individuals, including Nazi officials who often turned a blind eye to his activities due to the profits he generated for them. Despite his business dealings with the Nazis, Schindler found himself increasingly repulsed by their ideology and began contemplating ways he could help the Jewish population.

As the mass deportations and killings of Jews escalated, Schindler orchestrated a plan to protect his Jewish workers from certain death. By bribing and manipulating Nazi officials, he obtained permission to establish a subcamp of the Plaszow concentration camp, saving his workers from being transferred to even harsher conditions. The subcamp, which became known as "Schindler's List," provided a haven where Jewish workers were relatively safe from the horrors of the Holocaust. Schindler went to great lengths to secure the well-being of these workers, often at his personal expense and by risking his own life.

Schindler's transition from a profiteering industrialist to a savior of human lives remains a testament to his remarkable transformation and personal growth. His factory served not only as a place of business but also as a refuge, where he shielded his workers from the brutalities of the concentration camps. Schindler's commitment to protecting his Jewish employees went beyond what was expected or required by the circumstances. He initiated negotiations with Nazi officials, pleading for the lives of his workers and engaging in cunning tactics to subvert the system and ensure their survival.

The importance of Schindler's actions during this dark period of history cannot be overstated. By valuing human life over profit, he demonstrated the potential for individuals to make a significant difference in the face of immense evil. Schindler's story serves as an inspiration for generations to come, highlighting the power of empathy, courage, and resilience in the face of adversity. It reminds us to question the prevailing norms and challenge oppressive systems, even within the constraints of business and entrepreneurship. Rather, they became a platform for his heroic efforts to save the lives of over 1,200 Jewish workers. Schindler's enamelware factory and subsequent trading business allowed him to navigate the complex and morally compromised environment of Nazi-occupied Poland, enabling him to provide refuge and protection to those facing persecution and death. Schindler's story serves as a shining example of the power of one person's actions and the profound impact they can have on the lives of others. His legacy stands as a reminder of the importance of moral courage, selflessness, and the potential for individuals to make a difference in even the darkest of times.

Relationships with influential figures

One of the key aspects of cultivating relationships with influential figures is recognizing the immense value they bring to our lives. These figures possess knowledge, experience, and insights that can greatly benefit us. They may have achieved remarkable success in their respective fields, demonstrated exceptional leadership qualities, or possess deep expertise in specific areas. By connecting with them, we gain access to a treasure trove of wisdom and guidance, which can help us expand our horizons and make significant strides towards our own goals.

However, it is important to approach these relationships with a genuine desire to learn and grow, rather than seeking solely personal gain or validation. Influential figures are often busy individuals, with demands on their time and attention coming from various sources. Establishing a connection with them requires sincerity and a willingness to contribute to their lives and work as well. In order to build a strong relationship, it is vital to show respect for their time, value their expertise, and demonstrate a genuine interest in their endeavors.

Trust is the foundation of any healthy relationship, and this holds true for relationships with influential figures as well. Building trust takes time and consistent effort. It involves being reliable, maintaining confidentiality when necessary, and honoring commitments. By demonstrating integrity and honesty in our interactions, we can foster trust and create a solid foundation for these relationships to flourish.

Active engagement is another crucial element in nurturing relationships with influential figures. This involves seeking opportunities to connect and engage with them, whether it's attending conferences or events where they are speaking, participating in relevant online communities, or simply reaching out for a conversation or meeting. By actively pursuing these connections, we demonstrate our commitment to learning from them and benefiting from their experiences.

However, it's important to remember that these influential figures are not just sources of knowledge, but real people with emotions and personal lives. Genuine friendships can form through these relationships, and it is essential to show empathy and support for their personal and professional challenges. Taking an interest in their well-being and offering a helping hand when needed can strengthen these relationships beyond a professional connection.

Influential figures often appreciate individuals who show initiative and ambition. By demonstrating a proactive approach in our own personal and professional growth, we can establish ourselves as dedicated and motivated individuals. This can further enhance our connection with these figures, as they see our commitment to self-improvement and are more likely to invest in our growth and success.

Furthermore, as in any relationship, communication is key in cultivating relationships with influential figures. Effective communication involves active listening, expressing thoughts and ideas clearly, and seeking feedback when appropriate. By engaging in meaningful conversations, we not only gain valuable insights from these figures but also demonstrate our ability to contribute to thoughtful discussions. Establishing open lines of communication helps in building a strong rapport and demonstrating our commitment to growth and collaboration.

Lastly, gratitude plays a significant role in maintaining relationships with influential figures. By expressing sincere appreciation for their guidance and mentorship, we not only acknowledge their impact on our lives but also strengthen the bond between us. Taking the time to send a meaningful note, offering to help whenever possible, or even publicly acknowledging their influence can go a long way in nurturing these relationships. Navigating these relationships effectively requires sincerity, respect, trust, active engagement, empathy, initiative, effective communication, and gratitude. By embracing these principles, we can cultivate genuine connections and unlock the transformative power that these influential figures bring to our lives. So, let us embark on a journey of discovering and nurturing these vital relationships, and in doing so, unlock our true potential.

Acquisition of the Emalia factory

Before we dive into the acquisition itself, it is vital to understand the backdrop against which this event took place. In the early stages of World War II, Poland was invaded by Nazi Germany, and Krakow was promptly occupied. This occupation resulted in the establishment of the Krakow Ghetto, where thousands of Jews were forced to live in dire conditions. Amidst this bleak reality, Oskar Schindler, a German businessman with ties to the Nazi party, saw an opportunity to acquire the Emalia factory in Krakow, as it would offer him abundant production capabilities at a low cost.

In late 1939, Schindler seized this opportunity and, with financial support from Jewish entrepreneur Abraham Bankier, purchased the Emalia factory. Schindler's decision to acquire the factory was not entirely motivated by altruism or a desire to save lives at this stage. Instead, it was primarily a business move to exploit the abundant availability of cheap Jewish labor. Schindler's initial focus was on maximizing production and profit, without any indication of the transformative role he would later play in protecting the lives of his workers.

Once in possession of the factory, Schindler faced numerous challenges. The production of enamelware demanded a skilled workforce, and as he soon discovered, many of the Jewish workers brought to Emalia from the ghetto possessed the necessary skills. Recognizing their value, Schindler began to rely on their expertise and gradually built a relationship with them. Over time, he formed personal connections with individual workers, witnessing their suffering under the oppressive Nazi regime. These experiences sparked a change in Schindler's mindset and propelled him towards a newfound sense of compassion and determination to shield his workers from the horrors of the Holocaust.

Schindler's transformation into a savior of Jewish lives gained momentum in 1943 when the Emalia factory was scheduled for closure due to its inability to sustain profitable operations. In a remarkable and bold move, Schindler managed to negotiate an agreement with the German authorities, convincing them that the factory's production capabilities were essential for the war effort. This agreement allowed him to keep the factory running and, crucially, retain the Jewish workers who depended on it for survival.

With the relentless persecution and extermination of Jews unfolding around them, Schindler threw himself into protecting his workers from harm. He devised various strategies to ensure their safety, bribing officials, providing extra rations, and even relocating them to his newly established labor camp in Brunnlitz, Czechoslovakia. This action proved to be a pivotal turning point, as it transformed the Emalia factory workers into Schindlerjuden, a term used to describe the Jewish workers saved by Schindler throughout the war.

The acquisition of the Emalia factory, initially driven by financial motivation, turned into a story of immense courage and humanity. Oskar Schindler's decision to acquire the factory in Krakow, his subsequent recognition of the value and worth of his Jewish workers, and his relentless efforts to protect them from deportation and extermination are a testament to the power of individual actions, even in the face of overwhelming evil. From a profit-oriented businessman, Schindler transitioned into a hero who tirelessly worked to save the lives of his Jewish workers during the Holocaust. The backdrop of Nazi-occupied Poland and the grim reality of the Krakow Ghetto set the stage for this extraordinary story of compassion and bravery. The Emalia factory became a sanctuary for hundreds of Jews, shielding them from the horrors of the Holocaust and offering a glimmer of hope amidst the darkness. The story of Schindler's acquisition of the Emalia factory will forever serve as a testament to the indomitable spirit of humanity in the face of unimaginable cruelty.

CHAPTER 4: THE NAZI OCCUPATION

The impact of the Nazi regime on Schindler's business

The rise of Nazism in Germany led by Adolf Hitler in the 1930s brought about a radical transformation of the social, political, and economic landscape. Anti-Semitic sentiment became deeply ingrained in the Nazi ideology, culminating in the implementation of discriminatory laws targeting Jews. As the regime's grip on power tightened, Jews were systematically marginalized, stripped of their rights and properties, and eventually incarcerated in concentration camps. This hostile environment posed immense challenges for Jewish business owners, including Oskar Schindler.

Oskar Schindler, a German industrialist and opportunist, recognized the potential for profit that the Nazi regime's policies presented. He established an enamelware factory in Krakow, Poland, initially seeing an opportunity to exploit Jewish labor. However, as he became personally acquainted with the brutal treatment and dire circumstances faced by Jews, Schindler underwent a transformative realization. Witnessing firsthand the atrocities committed against the Jewish population, he felt compelled to intervene and help those he could.

The Nazi regime's impact on Schindler's business was

twofold. On the one hand, the regime's policies allowed Schindler to acquire Jewish labor at significantly reduced costs. The desperate and vulnerable position of Jewish workers in the labor market could be exploited for financial gain. Schindler's factory benefited from the availability of cheap labor, enabling him to produce goods at a lower cost and potentially increasing profits. This was a common strategy utilized by many businesses at the time, but for Schindler, it marked the beginning of a deeply personal and transformative journey.

On the other hand, the Nazi regime's persecution of Jews presented considerable risks and challenges for Schindler's business. The regime implemented strict regulations and controls on businesses, especially those employing Jews. Constant pressure and the ever-present threat of confiscation, closure, or punishment required delicate maneuvering to maintain operations. Schindler had to navigate a complex web of bureaucracy and corruption, employing various strategies to ensure the survival and functioning of his factory.

Schindler's factory became a haven for Jews amid the horrors of Nazi persecution. He went to great lengths to protect his workers from deportation to death camps, often leveraging his connections, charisma, and charm to secure their release. Schindler's efforts to save his Jewish workers were daring and courageous, often risking his own safety and reputation. He bribed Nazi officials, skillfully manipulated paperwork, and utilized his charisma to buy time and protection for those under his care.

The impact of the Nazi regime on Schindler's business, however, went beyond the financial and operational aspects. Schindler's actions highlight the power of individual agency and the capacity for moral courage in the face of unimaginable adversity. His remarkable transformation from a self-interested businessman to a savior of hundreds of Jewish lives showcases the potential for human decency amidst a period of profound darkness.

The story of Oskar Schindler and his factory is a testament to the resilience of the human spirit and serves as a reminder of the atrocities committed under the Nazi regime. It reminds us that even in the most challenging circumstances, there are opportunities for individuals to defy norms, challenge injustice, and protect the vulnerable. Schindler's actions have resonated with generations of people, inspiring countless acts of bravery and compassion. The regime's policies allowed Schindler to initially benefit from the exploitation of Jewish labor, but as he witnessed the suffering inflicted on the Jewish population, he made a conscious choice to step beyond his own self-interest and protect as many lives as possible. Schindler's story serves as a beacon of hope amidst the darkness of the Holocaust, demonstrating the profound impact that one person can have in the face of immense adversity.

Schindler's initial reactions to the persecution of Jews

In the early stages of the Nazi regime, Schindler, like many Germans, embraced the party's populist rhetoric and anti-Semitic propaganda. The portrayal of Jews as subhuman, responsible for Germany's economic struggles, and embodying an abstract enemy, found resonance with a significant portion of German society. Schindler, influenced by these prevailing sentiments, may have initially harbored bias against Jews as well. As an ambitious businessperson, he likely saw an opportunity to exploit the war for financial gain, particularly through the mass exploitation and mistreatment of Jews.

However, Schindler's outlook began to shift when he witnessed firsthand the horrific treatment and persecution of Jews in his role as an industrialist. The scenes of ghettoization, forced labor, and the abhorrent conditions they endured left a profound impact on him. It is crucial to note that Schindler's initial change of heart was not a rapid epiphany but rather a gradual process shaped by personal experiences. As he interacted with Jews who worked in his factories or came into contact with those affected by Nazi policies, he started to question the validity and morality of the Nazi ideology.

One pivotal event that added fuel to Schindler's growing dissent occurred when he witnessed the liquidation of the Kraków Ghetto. The brutality and callousness exhibited by the Nazi forces during this operation deeply disturbed him. Witnessing the defenseless men, women, and children facing the wrath of their oppressors seemingly tore apart the remnants of any sympathy or support he might have had for the ideology he initially embraced. The sheer magnitude of this blatant discrimination and the extent of human suffering evoked a profound sense of outrage and a solemn realization that he needed to take action.

Schindler's transformation from a participant in the Nazi machinery to a compassionate savior was also influenced by his personal relationships with Jews. Through his interactions with Jewish individuals in his employ, he began to recognize their humanity and the undue persecution they faced. Schindler forged relationships, friendships even, with some of his Jewish workers, and this allowed him to empathize with their plight. Their stories of pain and loss touched him on a deeply personal level, inspiring a fervent desire to intervene and protect them from the fate befalling so many others.

Moreover, Schindler's initial observations of the systematic dehumanization and eventual annihilation of Jews also played an essential role in his transformation. Witnessing the efficient and merciless implementation of the "Final Solution" in concentration camps, such as Auschwitz, horrified Schindler. It demonstrated the ultimate consequences of the anti-Semitic ideology he once subscribed to, forcing him to confront the monstrosity he had tacitly supported.

In summary, Oskar Schindler's initial reactions to the persecution of Jews were likely influenced by the prevailing anti-Semitic sentiments of his time, as well as his personal ambition. However, witnessing the atrocities inflicted on Jews, particularly during the liquidation of the Kraków Ghetto, and developing personal relationships with Jewish individuals in his employ led to a profound change of heart. Schindler's transformation from a profiteer to a compassionate humanitarian was a gradual process, driven by a growing disillusionment with the Nazi ideology and a recognition of the humanity and injustice suffered by the Jewish people. These initial reactions set the stage for Schindler's subsequent heroic actions in saving the lives of thousands during the Holocaust.

The decision to take action

One factor that often hinders our decision to take action is fear. Fear of the unknown, fear of failure, and fear of what others may think often holds us back from pursuing our goals and dreams. However, it is important to remember that fear is a natural response to change and uncertainty. Acknowledging our fears and understanding that they are a normal part of the decision-making process can help us move past them. Taking small steps towards our goals and embracing a growth mindset can also aid in overcoming fear, as we learn to view challenges as opportunities for growth and development.

Another factor that significantly influences our decision to take action is our mindset. Having a positive and proactive mindset can empower us to take charge of our lives and embrace new opportunities. On the other hand, a negative mindset can leave us feeling helpless and stuck in a state of inaction. By cultivating a growth mindset, where we view setbacks as temporary and work through challenges with resilience and determination, we can increase our likelihood of taking meaningful actions towards our goals.

Furthermore, the decision to take action is often influenced by external factors, such as societal expectations, cultural norms, and the opinions of others. It is important to be aware of these influences and the potential impact they may have on our decisions. While seeking advice and input from others can be valuable, it is crucial to remember that ultimately, we are the ones who will have to live with the consequences of our decisions. Taking the time to reflect on our values, priorities, and long-term aspirations can help us determine the best course of action for ourselves, regardless of external pressures.

To make effective decisions and take meaningful action, it is important to gather and evaluate information. This process of gathering information can involve conducting research, seeking advice from experts, and gathering firsthand experiences to ensure that we have a comprehensive understanding of the situation at hand. It is also helpful to consider potential risks and benefits, as well as the short-term and long-term implications of our choices. By taking a systematic and analytical approach, we can make informed decisions that are aligned with our goals and values.

Once we have gathered and evaluated information, it is important to set clear and achievable goals. By defining our objectives, we create a roadmap that guides our actions and keeps us focused on what matters most. Setting specific, measurable, attainable, relevant, and time-bound (SMART) goals can help us stay motivated and ensure that our actions are aligned with our desired outcomes.

In short, taking action requires persistence and a willingness to adapt. It is important to recognize that not all decisions will lead to immediate success, and setbacks are a natural part of the process. By approaching challenges with a flexible mindset and learning from our mistakes, we can adjust our strategies and persevere towards our goals. It is also essential to celebrate small victories along the way and acknowledge our progress, as this can boost our motivation and confidence. By understanding the factors that influence our decisions, cultivating a positive mindset, gathering and evaluating information, setting clear goals, and embracing persistence and adaptability, we can make informed and effective choices. While the path forward may not always be clear, it is important to remember that inaction can hold us back from reaching our full potential. By taking action, we open ourselves up to new possibilities and opportunities for growth. So, let us embrace the decision to take action and embark on the path towards a more fulfilling and successful future.

CHAPTER 5: SCHINDLER'S LIST

Compilation of the list

Firstly, it is essential to determine the purpose and scope of your list. Are you trying to keep track of the items you need to buy at the grocery store. Or perhaps you are creating a comprehensive inventory of all the equipment in your office. Clearly defining the objective of your list will guide your selection of items and ensure that nothing important is overlooked.

Once you have established the purpose of your list, it is important to prioritize the items you wish to include. This step involves assessing the urgency or importance of each item and arranging them in a logical order. For instance, if you are creating a list of tasks to complete for a project, you might consider putting the most time-sensitive tasks at the top of the list. By prioritizing items, you can ensure that your attention is focused on the most crucial aspects first.

Another crucial aspect of list compilation is organization. A well-organized list is easier to navigate and allows you to find items quickly and efficiently. There are several methods you can employ to organize your list, depending on its nature. For example, if you are making a list of references for a research paper, you might choose to organize them alphabetically by the author's surname. On the other hand, if you are creating a list of items to pack for a vacation, you could group them by category, such as clothing, toiletries, and electronics. By organizing your list, you can save time and avoid the frustration of searching for specific items.

Furthermore, it is crucial to regularly update your list to reflect any changes or new information. Lists are not static entities; they should evolve as circumstances change. For instance, if you are creating a list of goals for the year, it is important to review and update them periodically to ensure they remain relevant and aligned with your current priorities. By updating your list regularly, you can maintain accuracy and ensure that your list continues to serve its purpose effectively.

In addition to the aforementioned principles, there are several practical tips and techniques that can enhance your list compilation process. One such tip is to keep your list concise and focused. Including too many items or irrelevant information can clutter your list and make it less effective. Additionally, consider using clear and specific language when describing items on your list to avoid any confusion or ambiguity.

Another useful technique is to utilize technology to create and manage your lists. There are numerous apps and software available that can help you create digital lists, set reminders, and even share your lists with others. Digital lists offer the advantage of being easily editable and accessible from multiple devices, ensuring that you have your list with you wherever you go.

Lastly, it is important to approach the act of list-making with a positive mindset. Lists can be powerful tools for organization and efficiency, but they can also be overwhelming if approached with a negative attitude. Instead of viewing your list as a daunting collection of tasks or responsibilities, try to perceive it as a tool that will help you stay focused and productive. Celebrate your progress as you check items off your list, and use it as a source of motivation to accomplish your goals. By determining the purpose and scope of your list, prioritizing items, organizing your list, regularly updating it, and employing practical tips and techniques, you can create effective and efficient lists that serve their intended purpose. Remember to approach list-making with a positive mindset and view it as a helpful tool rather than a burden. With these strategies in mind, you can become a master of list compilation and experience the benefits of improved organization and productivity in your daily life.

Negotiations with Nazi officials

The motivations behind negotiations with Nazi officials varied depending on the context and the individuals or entities involved. In some cases, negotiations were driven by a genuine belief that diplomacy and compromise could prevent further bloodshed and lead to a peaceful resolution. This belief was often shared by diplomats and politicians who hoped that by engaging in dialogue, they could influence the Nazis and mitigate their destructive ambitions. However, it is critical to acknowledge that these motivations were not always based on sound judgment or a comprehensive understanding of the Nazi regime's true intentions.

Challenges in negotiations with Nazi officials were numerous and multifaceted. Firstly, it is vital to acknowledge the immense power wielded by the Nazi regime during their era. Negotiating with such a powerful and ideologically rigid regime presented significant obstacles, as the Nazis were notorious for their brutal tactics and ruthless pursuit of their objectives. They often used negotiations as a means to buy time, manipulate opponents, or gain a strategic advantage. This made it exceedingly difficult for negotiating parties to discern whether they were dealing with genuine intentions or mere deception.

Another challenge lay in the moral quandary of negotiating with a regime responsible for atrocities and human rights abuses on an unprecedented scale. The negotiations inevitably raised profound ethical questions, putting diplomats, politicians, and representatives under intense scrutiny. Critics rightly questioned whether engaging in negotiations with Nazi officials legitimized their actions or compromised the pursuit of justice. These ethical considerations speak to the heart of the challenges faced by those involved in negotiations with the Nazi regime.

To navigate negotiations with Nazi officials successfully, it was imperative to strike a delicate balance between maintaining one's moral principles and achieving tangible results. Skilled negotiators understood that any agreement with the Nazis needed to be approached with great caution, requiring meticulous attention to detail and a clear understanding of the regime's true motives. Furthermore, establishing red lines and non-negotiables was crucial to prevent crossing an ethical threshold. An approach that emphasized firmness while leaving room for possible concessions allowed negotiators to maintain credibility while potentially securing favorable outcomes that would benefit the wider population.

Despite these challenges, there were instances where negotiations with Nazi officials yielded positive outcomes. An example of this can be found in the famous case of Swedish diplomat Raoul Wallenberg, who saved tens of thousands of Jews during World War II. While not directly negotiating with high-ranking Nazi officials, Wallenberg skillfully used diplomacy, subtle negotiations, and deception to rescue Jewish individuals and provide them with false documentation, ultimately saving countless lives. This case highlights the potential effectiveness of negotiations, even in the face of an extremist regime like the Nazis.

In considering negotiations with Nazi officials, it is crucial to avoid a simplified black-and-white perspective. While some negotiations may have been perceived as morally reprehensible, it is essential to examine each case within its historical context and recognize the complexities at play. By doing so, we gain a more comprehensive understanding of the decisions made at the time and the difficult choices confronted by those involved. Critically analyzing these negotiations allows us to reflect on the lessons learned and the implications for diplomacy and negotiation in the face of aggressors and human rights violators in the present and future. Understanding the motivations behind such negotiations, the challenges faced, and the ethical considerations involved is crucial for comprehending the decisions made during this dark period in history. Through a nuanced examination of this topic, we ensure that the mistakes of the past are not forgotten, that the victims are remembered, and that we learn valuable lessons to shape a more just and peaceful future.

The first group of Jews saved by Schindler

To understand the gravity of the situation faced by these Jews, it is essential to examine the historical context in which their story unfolds. The Nazis, under Adolf Hitler's leadership, had launched a systematic campaign of discrimination, persecution, and ultimately extermination against Jews across Europe. This policy aimed at the annihilation of an entire people, motivated by a fanatical ideology rooted in anti-Semitism. The Jews of Poland, in particular, bore the brunt of this brutal onslaught, with ghettos and death camps sprouting across the country. Amidst this chaos, Oskar Schindler, a German industrialist and member of the Nazi party, stepped forward to protect those he employed.

Schindler's journey to becoming a rescuer of Jews was not immediate nor linear. As a businessman, he initially saw the war as an opportunity for personal gain, seizing numerous enterprises in Poland. However, over time, he witnessed the atrocities perpetrated by the Nazis and grew disillusioned with their ideology. The tipping point for him came when he witnessed the liquidation of the Krakow ghetto in March 1943. The sight of thousands of Jews being forcibly removed from their homes and sent to death camps left an indelible mark on Schindler's conscience. From that point forward, he resolved to do whatever he could to protect his Jewish workforce.

The decision to inextricably tie his fate with that of his Jewish employees was not without risks. Schindler exploited his connections with Nazi officials, using bribery and charm to secure the transfer of as many workers as possible to his own factory. He portrayed the workers as indispensable, convincing the authorities that they were essential for the war effort. Through these tactics, he managed to establish a sanctuary within the walls of his factory, where Jews could find refuge from the horrors outside. The first group saved by Schindler constituted a diverse mix of individuals, including skilled workers, intellectuals, and families. They shared a common fate, facing the horrors of the Holocaust but given a glimmer of hope through their association with Schindler.

Life within the walls of Schindler's factory was far from idyllic, yet it provided a stark contrast to the relentless suffering endured by those in the ghettos and camps. In the factory, Schindler ensured that his Jewish workers received adequate food and shelter, often at great personal expense. He shielded them from the arbitrary cruelty inflicted by Nazi overseers, intervening whenever possible to prevent their abuse. The workers, fully aware of the precariousness of their situation, reciprocated Schindler's actions with profound gratitude and loyalty. The bond that formed between Schindler and his workers was a testament to the power of compassion and shared suffering.

The first group saved by Schindler managed to survive until 1945 when the Soviet army liberated Krakow from Nazi control. As the war drew to a close, Schindler arranged for his workers to be transferred to the relative safety of his homeland, Germany. He provided them with forged documents, ensuring that they would not be subjected to further persecution. These actions went against the tide, as many Nazis sought to eliminate any evidence of their crimes. Schindler, however, remained steadfast in his commitment to saving as many lives as possible. Schindler's remarkable transformation from a profit-driven opportunist to a selfless rescuer stands as a shining example of the power of conscience and compassion. Through his efforts, 1,200 individuals were given a chance at life, while countless others now hold the memory of his heroism close to their hearts. The first group saved by Schindler represents not only a one in history but a powerful reminder of our shared responsibility to safeguard the dignity and lives of our fellow human beings.

CHAPTER 6: LIFE IN THE KRAKOW GHETTO

Conditions in the ghetto

One of the most pressing issues within the ghettos was the severe overcrowding. Jewish families were forcibly relocated to these designated areas, often encompassing small sections of cities or towns. The limited space available was simply inadequate to accommodate the vast number of people packed into these confined areas. Families were crammed into small apartments or shared rooms, with minimal privacy or personal space. This overcrowding not only led to immense physical discomfort but also contributed to the spread of diseases and illnesses, further exacerbating the already dire conditions.

Another distressing aspect of life in the ghettos was the lack of basic necessities. The Jewish population was subjected to severe food and water shortages. Rations were allocated to the ghettos by the German authorities, but these amounts were grossly inadequate. People were constantly plagued by hunger, and many resorted to desperate measures to survive. The scarcity of clean water also posed significant health risks, leading to the spread of waterborne diseases and further deteriorating the living conditions.

Living conditions in the ghettos were further compounded by the lack of adequate sanitation facilities. The already limited resources were insufficient to support the sheer number of individuals confined within the ghettos. As a result, proper waste disposal mechanisms were non-existent or woefully inadequate. This led to unsanitary conditions, with trash piling up and sewage systems failing. The lack of hygiene and sanitation had severe implications for public health, with outbreaks of diseases such as typhus and dysentery sweeping through the already vulnerable population.

In addition to the physical hardships, the psychological toll on individuals living in the ghettos cannot be underestimated. The conditions imposed by the Nazi regime were intentionally dehumanizing, aiming to crush the spirits of those subjected to it. Individuals were stripped of their dignity and forced to endure constant fear and humiliation. The constant presence of armed guards and the threat of violence loomed over the ghetto residents, instilling a sense of powerlessness and despair. The psychological trauma inflicted upon the Jewish population lingers even today, serving as a stark reminder of the atrocities committed during this dark one of history.

Resistance within the ghettos, though often difficult and dangerous, nonetheless emerged as a way for the residents to assert their humanity and preserve their dignity. Collective acts of defiance, such as the clandestine production of literature, art, and music, served as powerful forms of resistance against the oppression and dehumanization. These acts provided a much-needed outlet for expression and creativity, allowing individuals to momentarily transcend their grim surroundings. Through these acts of resistance, the residents of the ghettos were able to maintain some semblance of hope and resilience in the face of unimaginable adversity.

It is essential that we remember and reflect on the

conditions in the ghettos as a reminder of the importance of justice, compassion, and equality. The atrocities committed within the ghettos during World War II serve as a chilling warning against the dangers of discrimination and marginalization. By acknowledging and understanding these historical injustices, we can strive to build a world that values the inherent worth and dignity of every individual, irrespective of their background or identity. Overcrowding, lack of basic necessities, inadequate sanitation, and psychological trauma were all part of the harrowing reality faced by those confined within the ghettos. Amidst the darkness, acts of resistance and resilience emerged, serving as symbols of hope in the face of unimaginable suffering. Remembering and learning from the conditions in the ghettos can inspire us to create a world where the principles of justice and equality prevail, ensuring that such atrocities are never repeated.

Schindler's interactions with residents

One striking aspect of Schindler's interactions was his ability to establish personal connections with the residents. Despite being a member of the Nazi party, Schindler displayed empathy and compassion towards the Jews under his protection. He forged relationships with them, learning about their backgrounds, families, and aspirations. These interactions went beyond the surface level, allowing Schindler to understand the individual struggles and fears of the people he was helping. By treating them as individuals rather than merely a collective group, Schindler demonstrated a profound respect for the residents and their humanity.

Schindler's interactions with residents extended beyond the workplace, as he often intervened to protect them from the brutality of the Nazi regime. He used his connections and persuasive skills to shield his workers from deportations to concentration camps. Schindler skillfully maneuvered through the bureaucratic machinery of the Nazi system, leveraging his influence to ensure the safety of those under his care. Personal relationships and connections with authorities played a crucial role in this aspect of his interactions, as Schindler often had to negotiate and persuade others to release individuals or prevent their arrests. These interactions highlight Schindler's resourcefulness and determination to protect the lives of those entrusted to him.

Another dimension of Schindler's interactions with residents was his involvement in their daily lives and well-being. He went beyond the role of an employer by providing additional support to the people he employed. Schindler ensured that his workers had access to basic necessities such as food, shelter, and medical care, despite the challenges of wartime scarcity. He often went to great lengths to secure supplies for his employees, even making deals with other officials to acquire what was necessary. These interactions exemplify Schindler's commitment to not only saving lives but also alleviating the suffering of those impacted by the war. His dedication to their well-being created a sense of trust and loyalty among the residents, cementing their reliance on him as a protector and ally.

Schindler's interactions with non-Jewish residents also revealed a complex dynamic. While there were instances where tensions arose due to conflicts of interest or prejudices, Schindler often managed to bridge the divide. He leveraged his charm, influence, and persuasive abilities to foster collaboration and unity within his community. By emphasizing the shared humanity and common goals among residents, Schindler consciously worked to dismantle the barriers that divided them. He forged alliances, developed friendships, and ultimately united people from different backgrounds, demonstrating his ability to harmonize diverse groups under challenging circumstances.

The impact of Schindler's interactions with residents cannot be understated. His actions saved countless lives and provided hope in a time of despair. Through personal connections, protection from persecution, and support beyond the workplace, Schindler demonstrated the power of individual agency and compassion in the face of unimaginable adversity. His interactions showcased the ability of one person to make a difference, inspiring others to take action and challenging the prevailing narrative of indifference during the Holocaust. Through personal connections, strategic interventions, and involvement in the daily lives of the people he employed, Schindler displayed empathy, resourcefulness, and a fierce determination to resist the horrors of the Nazi regime. His interactions with the residents reveal a multifaceted character who defied expectations and channeled his power and influence towards the greater good. Schindler's story serves as a testament to the power of compassion and the profound impact one person can have in the face of unimaginable darkness.

The decision to move Jews to the Plaszow labor camp

To comprehend the decision to move Jews to the Plaszow labor camp, it is crucial to understand the broader historical backdrop against which it unfolded. By the time Plaszow was established, the Nazis had already set in motion their horrific plan to eradicate the Jewish population. The ideology of Adolf Hitler and his Nazi regime was built upon a foundation of anti-Semitism and racial superiority, which sought to cleanse Europe of Jews through systematic discrimination, persecution, and ultimately, mass murder. Thus, the choice to create Plaszow specifically for Jewish forced labor was consistent with this genocidal agenda, as it provided a means to exploit and further marginalize the Jewish population.

The motive behind moving Jews to Plaszow was multidimensional and intertwined with the Nazis' overall strategy of domination and extermination. While the creation of labor camps had, in a sense, presented an opportunity for the Nazis to exploit Jewish labor for their war effort, it also served another insidious purpose. As the Nazi regime systematically stripped Jews of their rights, property, and freedom, the Plaszow labor camp became a tool to exert greater control and impose further suffering on an already persecuted populace. Confining Jews within a single camp facilitated the Nazis' manipulation and manipulation, allowing them to orchestrate a regime of terror and systematic abuse.

Moreover, the decision to move Jews to the Plaszow labor camp exemplified the Nazis' penchant for using bureaucratic mechanisms to streamline their oppressive machinery. The establishment of Plaszow represented a shift from makeshift ghettos and temporary camps to a more organized and permanent structure, embodying a more efficient logistical framework for the Nazis' persecution and exploitation of Jews. By consolidating the Jewish population at Plaszow, the Nazis were able to exert centralized control, making it easier to manage the labor force, monitor and restrict movement, and maintain tighter surveillance. This move was not only a reflection of the Nazis' desire for control but also their commitment to establishing a comprehensive infrastructure for the persecution and ultimate extermination of European Jewry.

The impact of the decision to move Jews to the Plaszow labor camp on those who were subjected to it cannot be overstated. For thousands of Jews, this relocation marked the beginning of an unimaginable ordeal characterized by constant terror, dehumanization, and rampant abuse. The conditions at Plaszow were exceedingly harsh, with prisoners subjected to forced labor, starvation, arbitrary executions, and sadistic acts of violence perpetrated by the commandant, Amon Göth. The infamous "liquidation" of the Krakow ghetto in March 1943 resulted in the transfer of thousands of Jews to Plaszow, leading to further overcrowding and exacerbating the grim living conditions.

The camp's location near Krakow also had significant ramifications. Krakow, a city with a rich Jewish heritage, had become a vital center of Jewish life and culture in pre-war Poland. Its vibrant Jewish community engendered a sense of identity and strength among its members. However, the decision to move Jews to Plaszow stripped them of this connection to their roots, fracturing communities and further isolating individuals from their support networks. For many, the move to Plaszow meant leaving behind loved ones, observing the destruction of their neighborhoods, and witnessing the erasure of their cultural and religious practices.

The decision to move Jews to the Plaszow labor camp reflects the dark depths humanity can sink to when consumed by hatred and prejudice. It epitomizes the extent to which the Nazi regime was willing to go in their quest for domination and supremacy. Far from being a mere administrative choice, this decision represented a pivotal moment in the Holocaust, where the Nazis demonstrated their unwavering commitment to the dehumanization, exploitation, and ultimately, the genocide of the Jewish people. Examining this topic allows for a greater understanding of the multifaceted motives behind the decision, and enables us to bear witness to the unimaginable suffering endured by those trapped within the confines of Plaszow. Only through remembering and understanding these atrocities can we strive to prevent such horrors from recurring in the future.

CHAPTER 7: PLASZOW LABOR CAMP

Aktion Krakau

In order to fully understand the context of Aktion Krakau, it is necessary to delve into the broader historical backdrop of Nazi Germany. Adolf Hitler and his Nazi party rose to power in Germany in 1933, and it wasn't long before they began implementing their radical racial policies. These policies were largely based on the concept of Aryan supremacy, which sought to establish the superiority of the so-called Aryan race, and condemned Jews as a threat to the master race.

Krakow, a city in southern Poland, had a significant Jewish population during this period. In fact, it was one of the cultural and intellectual centers of Jewish life in Eastern Europe. However, with the rise of Nazi ideology, the Jews of Krakow became subject to increasing discrimination, persecution, and ultimately, extermination.

Aktion Krakau began on June 22, 1940, and lasted for two days. It was one of the earliest instances of large-scale deportations of Jews to concentration camps, specifically to the newly established Auschwitz concentration camp, which was located in close proximity to Krakow. The operation targeted approximately 3,000 Jewish men between the ages of 18 and 60, who were considered capable of physical labor by the Nazis.

During Aktion Krakau, the Nazis used various methods to apprehend and deport the Jewish men. They conducted door-to-door searches, raided homes, and utilized force whenever necessary. Once captured, the Jewish men were gathered at assembly points, where they were often subjected to brutality and humiliation. From there, they were transported to Auschwitz in packed trains, enduring long and arduous journeys under horrific conditions.

Upon arrival at Auschwitz, the fate of the Jewish men differed from many other concentration camps. Instead of immediate extermination, some were temporarily spared and assigned to forced labor details. Their labor was utilized by the Nazis for various purposes, including infrastructure projects and the production of war-related materials. However, it is important to note that the conditions in Auschwitz were still incredibly harsh and life expectancy was tragically low.

Aktion Krakau marked the beginning of a long and tragic one in the history of Krakow's Jewish community. The subsequent years saw a rapid deterioration of living conditions for the remaining Jews, culminating in the liquidation of the Krakow Ghetto in March 1943. The majority of the Jews who hadn't already been deported were then sent to death camps, where they met their tragic end.

The importance of remembering and studying Aktion Krakau extends beyond simply understanding the historical events themselves. It serves as a stark reminder of the consequences of unchecked hatred, discrimination, and prejudice. By learning about the atrocities committed during this operation, we can strive to ensure that such acts are never repeated in the future.

As we reflect on the events of Aktion Krakau, it is crucial to honor the memory of those who perished. This can be achieved through various means, such as preserving and visiting Holocaust memorials, engaging in educational discussions, and supporting organizations that promote tolerance and understanding. It is our collective responsibility to ensure that the horrors of the past are never forgotten and that we work towards a world of inclusivity and acceptance for all. It marked the beginning of a systematic approach to the extermination of Jews, showcasing the brutal and discriminatory policies of Nazi Germany. By studying and remembering Aktion Krakau, we can learn from the past and strive towards a future free from hatred and prejudice.

The brutality of SS officer Amon Goeth

Serving as the commandant of the Płaszów concentration camp, Goeth's name has become synonymous with acts of unspeakable brutality and suffering inflicted upon innocent victims. In this one, we shall delve into the life and actions of Amon Goeth, aiming to shed light on the depths of his depravity and explore the factors that contributed to his unimaginable crimes. By understanding the dark legacy left behind by Goeth, we can further comprehend the magnitude of the atrocities committed during this harrowing episode in human history.

Background and Rise to Power:
Born on December 11, 1908, in Vienna, Austria, Amon Goeth's childhood was marked by a tumultuous family life and a series of delinquencies. His inclination towards sadism and violence first emerged during his teenage years, foreshadowing the dark path he was bound to

traverse. In the early 1930s, Goeth aligned himself with the Nazi Party, drawn to its philosophy of supremacy and anti-Semitic ideals. With the advent of World War II, Goeth's loyalty and enthusiasm for the Nazi cause propelled his ascent through the SS ranks, ultimately culminating in his appointment as the commandant of the Płaszów concentration camp near Kraków, Poland, in 1943.

The Płaszów Concentration Camp:
Within the confines of the Płaszów camp, Goeth exercised absolute power, his sadistic tendencies unleashed upon countless victims. Inmates endured grueling labor, torture, and starvation, living in constant fear of Goeth's arbitrary cruelty. One particularly chilling aspect of Goeth's reign was the implementation of a "sport," wherein he would randomly shoot prisoners from his villa balcony, turning their lives into mere objects for his amusement. Goeth's reign was marked by a complete disregard for human life and a sadistic pleasure derived from inflicting pain.

The Kraków Ghetto Liquidation and Goeth's Role:
Goeth's brutality reached new heights during the liquidation of the Kraków Ghetto, which occurred between March and May 1943. With the help of his subordinate, SS-Hauptsturmführer Julian Scherner, Goeth orchestrated the mass deportation and extermination of thousands of Jewish men, women, and children from the ghetto. His unyielding determination to eliminate any trace of Jewish existence was evident in his ruthless methods, such as surrounding himself with vicious attack dogs trained to tear prisoners apart on command. Through his active involvement in the destruction of the Kraków Ghetto, Goeth cemented his status as a relentless instrument of Nazi terror.

The "Schindler's List" Connection:
One aspect that further amplifies the infamy of Amon Goeth

is his portrayal in Steven Spielberg's iconic film "Schindler's List." Liam Neeson's depiction of Oskar Schindler's efforts to save Jews from the clutches of Goeth provides a stark contrast between Goeth's malevolence and Schindler's extraordinary acts of compassion. The film brilliantly captures Goeth's sadistic nature, emphasizing the sheer depravity of the Holocaust through the eyes of those who witnessed it firsthand. "Schindler's List" remains a testament to the human capacity for both extraordinary evil and extraordinary goodness.

The Trial and Execution:
Following the end of World War II, Goeth went into hiding, but his capture in May 1945 signaled the beginning of his reckoning. In August 1946, he faced trial for his war crimes and atrocities committed at Płaszów. The prosecution presented compelling evidence, including testimonies from survivors who shared their horrific experiences under Goeth's command. Ultimately, the court found him guilty of multiple counts of murder, extermination, and cruelty, resulting in Goeth's death sentence. On September 13, 1946, Amon Goeth was hanged in Kraków, yet his legacy of cruelty and terror lingers on.

The brutality of SS Officer Amon Goeth serves as a haunting reminder of the depths to which human beings can descend when blinded by ideology and consumed by hatred. The magnitude of his crimes, characterized by his sadistic pleasure in inflicting suffering, showcases the extreme evil that prevailed during the Holocaust. Goeth's legacy underscores the importance of acknowledging these atrocities, ensuring that they remain etched in our collective memory as a stark warning against the repetition of such horrors. It is through understanding, remembrance, and continued education that we can strive to prevent the recurrence of such atrocities in our world.

Schindler's efforts to protect his workers

One of Schindler's most prominent methods of protecting his workers was through bribery. By establishing close relationships with high-ranking Nazi officials, he was able to secure numerous privileges for his factory and its employees. Schindler used his charm and persuasive skills to convince these officials that his factory was vital to the war effort, persuading them to offer a level of protection that most other Jews did not enjoy. He would frequently give expensive gifts or provide substantial monetary bribes in exchange for the safety of his workers. Through these underhanded tactics, Schindler ensured that his workers were shielded from deportation to concentration camps and the accompanying grim fate that awaited them.

In addition to bribery, Schindler employed deception as a key tool in protecting his workers. He created an atmosphere of indispensability around his factory, convincing the Nazi regime that his production of armaments was crucial to the war effort. This allowed him to maintain a certain level of autonomy and control over his workforce. Schindler skillfully utilized this autonomy to issue false documentation, forging identification papers and altering lists to remove names of potential victims of the Holocaust. By falsifying these crucial documents, he could shield his workers from the attention of the SS and other Nazi authorities who sought to eradicate the Jewish population. This strategy of deception played a significant role in the preservation of numerous lives under his watchful eye.

Moreover, Schindler's efforts to protect his workers extended beyond mere deception and bribery. He established a network of connections with sympathetic individuals who shared his desire to save lives. Schindler collaborated with the Jewish underground resistance, providing financial support and resources to help them smuggle people out of the ghettos and into his factory. He also employed skilled workers who were deemed essential to the production process but were at risk of deportation. By employing these individuals, Schindler skillfully used their talents as justification for their exemption from the grasp of the Nazi regime. This intricate network of cooperation and mutual aid played a pivotal role in the preservation of lives throughout his enterprise.

Schindler's dedication in protecting his workers extended well beyond the confines of his factory. He frequently put his own life on the line by intervening in acts of violence against Jewish individuals. His bravery and audacity in confronting Nazi soldiers who sought to harm or kill Jews were awe-inspiring. Schindler utilized his status and connections to intervene in perilous situations, often resorting to bluff and bluster to successfully extricate individuals from danger. These acts of personal intervention showcase the lengths to which Schindler was willing to go in order to safeguard the lives of his workers.

Ultimately, Schindler's efforts to protect his workers remain a shining example of how individual actions can make a monumental difference in the face of extreme adversity. His combination of resourcefulness, negotiation skills, and personal sacrifice enabled him to save the lives of over 1,200 people during one of the darkest periods in human history. Schindler's story serves as a reminder that even in the most dire circumstances, there is always the opportunity to act with empathy and courage. His legacy continues to inspire and challenge us, posing the question of what each of us would be willing to risk in order to safeguard the lives and dignity of others.

CHAPTER 8: THE ESCAPE

The liquidation of the camp

When discussing the liquidation of a concentration camp, it is important to recognize the immense loss of life and the egregious violations of human rights that occurred within their walls. These camps were places of unspeakable horrors, where innocent men, women, and children were subjected to systematic oppression, forced labor, and mass extermination. The liquidation process aimed to erase the evidence of these atrocities, obscuring the truth and attempting to deny the scale of the tragedy that unfolded.

One of the primary objectives in liquidating a concentration camp was to eradicate any traces of evidence that might implicate the perpetrators of these heinous crimes. Nazi officials were keenly aware of the international condemnation they would face if the full extent of their atrocities was revealed. By dismantling the camps and destroying any incriminating records or artifacts, they sought to cover up their actions and avoid accountability. However, through meticulous research and the testimonies of survivors, historians and human rights advocates have pieced together a comprehensive understanding of the atrocities committed within these camps.

The liquidation process itself was multifaceted, involving a range of tasks that needed to be coordinated and executed efficiently. First and foremost, the inmates of the camp had to be dealt with. In many cases, this involved the forced evacuation and deportation of prisoners to other camps or locations, often resulting in the loss of countless lives due to malnutrition, exhaustion, or outright brutality. These forced marches, known as "death marches," were yet another horrific one in the annals of the Holocaust, further highlighting the dehumanization and disregard for human life experienced by the captive populations.

Simultaneously, the physical infrastructure of the camps had to be dismantled. This included the destruction of barracks, crematoriums, and other structures that served as focal points for the systematic extermination of individuals deemed undesirable by the Nazis. How these structures were disposed of varied from camp to camp, with some being completely razed to the ground, while others were repurposed for different uses in a bid to erase the evidence of their original purpose.

The disposal of personal belongings and the wholesale destruction of any remaining evidence was also a vital part of the liquidation process. In scenes reminiscent of a dystopian nightmare, personal effects such as clothing, shoes, and personal documents were sorted and disposed of. This deliberate erasure of individuals' identities further emphasized the dehumanization that took place within the camps. These belongings represented not only the material possessions of the inmates but also the memories, hopes, and dreams of countless individuals whose lives were cut short by relentless persecution.

In the aftermath of the liquidation, the scars left by the concentration camp system were difficult to conceal. Mass graves, ashes, and the haunting remnants of these once bustling sites of terror served as haunting reminders of the horrors that took place. The slow process of decontamination and transformation of these spaces was essential to alleviate the psychological burden these locations represented. Institutions such as museums, memorials, and educational centers have worked tirelessly to ensure that the memories of those who perished are not forgotten, while also seeking to educate future generations about the dangers of hatred, discrimination, and genocide.

The liquidation of the camp is not just a historical event – it is a testament to the resilience of the human spirit, both in its capacity for immense evil and, more importantly, its ability to heal and seek justice. By understanding the process by which these camps were dismantled, we gain insight into the magnitude of the crimes committed, the herculean efforts required to uncover the truth, and the ongoing struggle to ensure that the victims are never forgotten. Through discussing the objectives, methods, and consequences of the liquidation process, we can better understand the scale of the atrocities committed within these camps and the complexities involved in uncovering and addressing the truth. By confronting this painful history, we honor the memories of the millions who suffered and perished and ensure that these crimes are never repeated.

Schindler's plan to rescue his workers

Schindler's journey to becoming a savior of Jewish lives began when he initially moved to Krakow, Poland, in 1939 to take advantage of the economic opportunities provided by the German occupation. Owning an enamelware factory, he soon realized the dire fate that awaited the Jews under Nazi rule. Witnessing firsthand the dehumanization and persecution of the Jewish population, Schindler was deeply moved and resolved to intervene.

One of the main components of Schindler's rescue plan

was to secure skilled Jewish workers for his factory. He recognized the value these individuals possessed and understood that their expertise was crucial to the success of his business. Consequently, he persuaded the German authorities to grant him permission to employ a workforce comprised of Jews, leveraging his connections and charisma to negotiate this unique arrangement. By presenting his factory as vital to the war effort and emphasizing the cost-effective advantages of utilizing Jewish labor, Schindler managed to save many lives by providing them with essential work permits.

Moreover, Schindler understood the importance of establishing strong relationships with Nazi officials and key figures in the Third Reich. This enabled him to exploit their vulnerabilities and protect his workers from deportation to the death camps. Schindler acted as a shield for his employees, utilizing his contacts to prevent their transfer to more dangerous locations like Auschwitz. His personal relationships with high-ranking SS officials such as Amon Goeth and Itzhak Stern allowed him to influence decisions and negotiate for the safety of his workers.

Schindler's strategy also involved bribing and providing gifts to Nazi officials. He used his acquired wealth, often spending exorbitant amounts, to secure favors and protection for his workers. These bribes ranged from luxury items like fine wines and cigars to monetary gifts that could alleviate the financial burdens faced by the officials. Through these acts of bribery, Schindler managed to keep his workforce intact and shield them from the clutches of death.

Furthermore, Schindler devised an ingenious plan to transfer his workers to a new factory in Brünnlitz, Czechoslovakia, as the Allies advanced and the Nazis implemented their "Final Solution." Recognizing that the relocation of his workers was an urgent priority, Schindler convinced the authorities that moving his factory would increase productivity and efficiency. This move not only prevented his workers from being transported to the extermination camps but also provided them with a safer environment in which they could continue their work.

Schindler's heroic and morally driven actions went beyond merely providing jobs and protection for his Jewish workers. He also went to great lengths to ensure their well-being, often at great personal risk. He provided his workers with food, medical care, and shelter, at times using his connections to smuggle essential supplies into the camp. Schindler displayed profound empathy and dedication to securing a better future for his workers, going beyond the call of duty to support and protect them during those dark times. By leveraging his influence, building relationships with Nazi officials, and using bribery when necessary, Schindler managed to save over a thousand Jews from the horrors of the Nazi death camps. His foresight, resourcefulness, and bravery demonstrate the extraordinary lengths one person can go to defy tyranny and fight for justice. Schindler's legacy serves as a timeless reminder of the power of compassion and the individual's ability to make a difference, even amid the darkest ones of history.

The journey to safety

In the realm of physical safety, individuals embark on a journey to shield themselves from dangers that threaten their well-being. This expedition often involves taking proactive measures to prevent potential harm and mitigate risks. We lock our doors at night, wear seatbelts while driving, and invest in security systems to safeguard our homes. Furthermore, society at large emphasizes safety through the implementation of laws and regulations, ensuring that public spaces and infrastructure meet certain standards. The journey to physical safety is not limited to our immediate surroundings; it extends to our travel and exploration of the world. We rely on safety measures such as traffic laws, airline safety procedures, and health precautions to minimize risks during our journeys. The continuous pursuit of physical safety reflects our innate instinct to protect ourselves and our loved ones from harm.

However, the journey to safety is not solely an external endeavor; it also entails finding solace within ourselves, an emotional and psychological sanctuary. In this aspect, safety becomes an internal state of mind, free from distress and anxiety. It is a place where we can find comfort and resilience in the face of adversity. This inner journey begins with recognizing and acknowledging our fears and insecurities. By developing self-awareness and understanding, we can address underlying issues that impede our emotional well-being. Self-care practices, such as meditation, exercise, and therapy, can be instrumental in navigating this path to self-assurance. Additionally, developing strong interpersonal connections and a support network allows us to create safe spaces within our relationships, where we can express ourselves authentically without fear of judgment or harm. The journey to emotional and psychological safety is an ongoing process of self-discovery and growth, as we learn to overcome our inner obstacles and cultivate resilience in the face of life's challenges.

Moreover, the quest for safety extends to the societal and communal level, where individuals strive to create environments that foster inclusivity, fairness, and security for everyone. This journey necessitates an understanding of the systemic inequalities and injustices that hinder safety for marginalized communities. It requires solidarity and collective action to challenge oppressive structures and create spaces where all individuals can thrive. Advocacy for social justice, equitable policies, and equal access to resources become essential components of the journey to safety at the communal level. This path calls upon individuals to educate themselves and engage in meaningful dialogue to challenge biases and dismantle systemic barriers. The journey to safety is not only about individual well-being; it is about creating a harmonious and secure society for all. It is a universal pursuit that resonates across cultures and time, driven by the innate human desire for security and well-being. This voyage requires an understanding of the external threats to our physical safety and the measures we can take to protect ourselves. Simultaneously, it demands an exploration of our internal landscape to find emotional and psychological solace. Furthermore, the journey to safety extends to society at large, where collective action is necessary to challenge systemic inequalities and create inclusive environments. Embarking on this journey requires continuous self-reflection, growth, and collaboration, as we strive to create a world where safety is not a privilege but a fundamental right for all.

CHAPTER 9: SCHINDLER'S LEGACY

Recognition of Schindler's actions

Oskar Schindler's remarkable actions during the Holocaust have garnered worldwide recognition and admiration. His courageous efforts to save over 1,000 Jews from certain death at the hands of the Nazis have immortalized him as a hero of unprecedented bravery. The recognition of Schindler's actions can be seen through various avenues, including the countless awards and accolades bestowed upon him and the enduring legacy he left behind.

One of the most prominent forms of recognition for Schindler's actions came in the form of the prestigious title of Righteous Among the Nations, bestowed by Yad Vashem, the World Holocaust Remembrance Center in Israel. This title is awarded to non-Jews who risked their lives to save Jews during the Holocaust, and is considered the highest honor for those involved in rescue efforts. Schindler was recognized as a Righteous Gentile in 1963, gaining worldwide attention and praise for his selfless acts. This official recognition not only solidified his heroic status but also ensured that his extraordinary deeds would be forever remembered.

In addition to being named a Righteous Among the Nations, Schindler received numerous other awards and honors for his actions during the Holocaust. In 1993, he was posthumously granted the title of Honorary Citizen of Israel, a rare distinction reserved for those who made extraordinary contributions to the state. This recognition further solidified Schindler's impact on Jewish history and the enduring gratitude felt by both the Jewish people and the nation of Israel.

Furthermore, Schindler's actions were adapted into the critically acclaimed and widely viewed film, Schindler's List, directed by Steven Spielberg. The film, released in 1993, not only brought Schindler's story to a global audience but also drew attention to the atrocities committed during the Holocaust. Spielberg's work not only shed light on the immense suffering endured by the Jewish people but also highlighted individuals like Schindler who risked everything to help others. The film received widespread acclaim and won seven Academy Awards, including Best Picture. This recognition further solidified Schindler's place in history and brought his heroic actions to the forefront of public consciousness.

Beyond official awards and media recognition, the recognition of Schindler's actions can also be seen in the countless testimonies and accounts from survivors whose lives were forever altered by his intervention. His selfless acts of bravery and empathy left an indelible mark on those he saved, as well as their families and future generations. Many survivors have spoken out about Schindler's unwavering determination to protect them, often referring to him as a savior and a true hero. Their personal accounts serve as powerful testament to the impact Schindler had on their lives and the gratitude they feel towards him.

Schindler's actions have resonated deeply with people from all walks of life, inspiring countless individuals to reflect on their own capacity for compassion and bravery. His story stands as a testament to the power of one person's actions to make a profound difference, even in the midst of unimaginable darkness. Schindler's recognition extends far beyond official titles and awards; it exists in the hearts and minds of those touched by his remarkable deeds. From being named a Righteous Among the Nations to receiving the title of Honorary Citizen of Israel, Schindler's heroic acts have been duly acknowledged by authoritative bodies. Furthermore, the success of the film adaptation of his story, Schindler's List, brought even broader recognition to his extraordinary deeds. Yet perhaps the most powerful recognition comes from the survivors themselves, who have lived to tell the world about Schindler's unwavering bravery and humanity. Schindler's legacy serves as a timeless reminder of the potential for good in every individual and continues to inspire countless others to make a positive difference in the face of adversity.

The impact on survivors

One of the most evident impacts on survivors is the physical toll that trauma can have on their bodies. In the immediate aftermath of a traumatic event, survivors might experience injuries, such as broken bones, cuts, or bruises. These physical wounds can be painful and may require medical intervention or long-term rehabilitation. Additionally, survivors may also suffer from internal injuries or develop chronic pain or diseases due to the stress and strain their bodies endured during the traumatic event.

However, the impact of trauma is not limited to physical injuries. Survivors often experience a range of mental and emotional effects, including heightened anxiety, depression, and post-traumatic stress disorder (PTSD). The psychological impact of trauma can be long-lasting and debilitating. Survivors may have flashbacks or nightmares, experience a persistent sense of fear or vulnerability, or find it challenging to trust others. These mental health challenges can interfere with their daily functioning, relationships, and overall quality of life.

Another critical aspect of the impact on survivors is the social effect that trauma can have. Relationships with family and friends may be strained, as survivors may struggle with expressing their emotions or may feel isolated and misunderstood. They may also face societal stigma or judgment, particularly if the traumatic event is linked to a contentious issue or perceived to be the survivor's fault. This can lead to feelings of shame, guilt, or even self-blame in some cases. It is crucial for society to provide support systems and opportunities for survivors to heal and reconnect with their communities.

Furthermore, the impact on survivors often extends beyond the immediate aftermath of a traumatic event. Some survivors may experience long-term consequences, such as chronic health conditions, disability, or financial hardships due to medical bills or loss of employment. The aftermath of trauma can also lead to substance abuse, self-destructive behavior, or even suicidal thoughts. It is essential to address these long-term impacts and provide survivors with ongoing support and resources to help them rebuild their lives.

In understanding the impact on survivors, it is crucial to acknowledge that individuals respond differently to traumatic events. Factors such as pre-existing mental health conditions, resilience, social support, and access to resources can significantly influence an individual's ability to cope and recover. Therefore, it is essential to adopt a holistic and individualized approach when providing support and treatment to survivors.

Various interventions and therapies have proven effective in addressing the impact on survivors. Cognitive-behavioral therapy (CBT), for example, has been found to help survivors manage anxiety and improve coping mechanisms. Eye Movement Desensitization and Reprocessing (EMDR) therapy, on the other hand, has been shown to be effective in treating PTSD by processing traumatic memories and reducing associated distress. Additionally, support groups and community-based programs can provide survivors with a sense of belonging, validation, and the opportunity to connect with others who have had similar experiences. Recognizing and addressing the diverse needs of survivors is crucial in helping them heal and rebuild their lives. By providing accessible and holistic support, society can mitigate the long-lasting effects of trauma and help survivors regain their sense of self, resilience, and hope for the future.

Schindler's post-war life

Following the conclusion of World War II in 1945, Schindler found himself in a vastly changed world. The revelations of the Holocaust and the unimaginable horrors endured by the Jewish people shook the global community. Schindler's own role in saving a significant number of Jews made him an enigmatic symbol of moral ambiguity. With the war's end, Schindler faced numerous challenges as he navigated the post-war world, both morally and financially. While many lauded his heroism during the war, others cast doubt on his motivation, questioning whether he acted purely out of altruism or for personal gain. This skepticism added an extra layer of complexity to Schindler's post-war life.

Financially destitute after the war, Schindler struggled to rebuild his life and overcome the economic upheaval brought on by Germany's defeat. The collapse of his businesses, including the famed enamelware factory in Krakow, left him with little to his name. Despite this setback, Schindler remained determined to support those who had survived the atrocities of the Holocaust. He utilized his network of connections and his charm to assist Jewish refugees in their journey towards a better life. Schindler's post-war life became intertwined with refugee and immigrant communities, providing him with a renewed sense of purpose amidst the chaos and despair of the post-war years.

Schindler's post-war efforts to aid Jewish refugees extended beyond financial support. He utilized his influence to secure travel documents and immigration permits, facilitating the emigration of survivors to various countries around the world. The establishment of the Brünnlitz factory in Czechoslovakia served as a focal point for these efforts. Schindler employed a significant number of Jewish refugees, offering them not only employment but also protection from the lingering anti-Semitism in the region. The factory became a sanctuary of sorts, where survivors found solace and the hope for a better future.

Despite his best efforts, Schindler faced challenges in adjusting to the moral and ethical dilemmas of his post-war life. The guilt and remorse he felt for not having done enough haunted him, leading him to addiction and emotional instability. He wrestled with the perception of himself as a hero, undermined by his Nazi Party affiliation and the transitional nature of his motivations. However, it is important to note that Schindler's post-war struggles did not define his legacy. His remarkable acts of bravery and empathy during the war remained a testament to the power of individual action in the face of overwhelming evil.

As the years passed, Schindler's post-war life took on a quieter tone. He retreated from the public eye, shying away from interviews and accolades. Instead, he focused on leading a more modest and introspective life. In 1974, he was recognized as one of the Righteous Among the Nations, an honor bestowed upon non-Jews who risked their lives to save Jews during the Holocaust. Schindler's inclusion on this prestigious list brought renewed attention and appreciation for his wartime heroism.

Schindler passed away on October 9, 1974, leaving behind a complex and enduring legacy. His heroism continues to inspire countless individuals, showcasing the profound impact that one person can have in a world plagued by hatred and prejudice. While his post-war life may have been marked by personal struggles and conflicts, Oskar Schindler's remarkable actions during the Holocaust will forever serve as a reminder of the capacity for compassion and bravery within us all. After saving over a thousand Jewish prisoners from the Holocaust, he faced numerous challenges, both financially and emotionally. Struggling to rebuild his life and reputation, Schindler dedicated himself to supporting Jewish refugees and ensuring their safety. His post-war efforts extended beyond financial aid, as he utilized his influence to secure travel documents and employment opportunities. Despite his struggles and internal conflicts, Schindler's heroism during the war remains a testament to the power of compassion and individual action. His story serves as a reminder of the indomitable spirit in the face of unimaginable evil.

CHAPTER 10: CONCLUSION

Lessons learned from his story

Their stories have the power to shape our perception, instill hope, and impart invaluable lessons that can guide us in our own lives. In this book, we delve into the lessons learned from one such remarkable story, wherein a man overcame adversity to achieve great success. By closely examining the experiences, trials, and triumphs of this individual, we aim to uncover valuable insights that can be applied to various aspects of our personal and professional lives.

The Power of Resilience
One profound lesson we draw from his story is the power of resilience in overcoming adversity. Throughout his journey, our protagonist encountered countless obstacles and setbacks. However, he refused to be defeated and instead used each setback as an opportunity for growth and development. He demonstrated the ability to bounce back from failures, learn from past mistakes, and adapt to changing circumstances. This resilience played a pivotal role in his ultimate triumph, reminding us that setbacks should not be viewed as failures but as stepping stones towards success, urging us to embrace our own challenges with unwavering determination.

Embracing Change and Adaptability
Another key lesson his story teaches us is the importance of embracing change and being adaptable in both personal

and professional spheres. The world is in a perpetual state of flux, and those who resist change often find themselves left behind. Our protagonist faced numerous unexpected changes throughout his journey, be it in the form of technological advancements, economic fluctuations, or shifting market demands. However, he displayed an extraordinary ability to embrace change, adjust his strategies, and reinvent himself when necessary. This lesson reminds us of the need to be open-minded, continuously learn, and be willing to adapt our approaches to thrive in an ever-evolving environment.

The Significance of Passion and Purpose
One of the most inspiring lessons derived from his story is the power of passion and purpose. Throughout his endeavors, our protagonist exemplified indomitable passion for what he believed in, and this unwavering commitment propelled him forward during the darkest moments. Furthermore, his story emphasizes the importance of aligning one's actions with a greater purpose. By pursuing a goal that extended beyond personal gain, he created a lasting impact on his community and became an exemplar of a life well-lived. This lesson serves as a reminder to identify our true passions and strive for a purpose that transcends mere success, ultimately leading to a more fulfilling and meaningful life.

The Role of Perseverance in Success
Perseverance is a trait that is deeply embedded in the fabric of our protagonist's story. Despite encountering setbacks, doubts, and challenges that seemed insurmountable, he never lost sight of his aspirations. His determination to keep moving forward, even in the face of seemingly insurmountable odds, is a testament to the power of perseverance. Through his relentless pursuit of success, our

protagonist teaches us that a strong work ethic, patience, and self-belief are essential ingredients in achieving our goals, reminding us that success rarely comes without perseverance.

The Value of Compassion and Collaboration
All in all, our hero's story illuminates the significance of compassion and collaboration in both personal and professional realms. His success was not solely a product of his own endeavors but was also intertwined with the support and collaboration of a diverse network of individuals. He valued the potential in others, nurtured relationships, and thrived in a culture of compassion and inclusivity. This crucial lesson teaches us that by fostering positive relationships, practicing empathy, and recognizing the strengths and contributions of those around us, we can achieve far greater success collectively than we ever could alone.

The lessons learned from his story transcend the realm of one individual's triumphs; they provide us with a valuable roadmap for navigating our own journeys. Through the power of resilience, adaptability, passion, perseverance, and compassion, we can overcome challenges, embrace change, find our purpose, achieve success, and forge lasting connections. By understanding and internalizing these lessons, we equip ourselves with the tools necessary to overcome obstacles and thrive in our personal and professional lives. Let this tale serve as both an inspiration and a practical guide to unleashing our potential and writing our own stories of triumph.

The importance of remembering the Holocaust and honoring the lives saved by Schindler

The act of remembering the Holocaust serves as a poignant and necessary reminder of the profound human capacity for evil. By reflecting on the horrors that unfolded during this period, we are confronted with the consequences of unchecked hatred, bigotry, and discrimination. It is only through remembering and understanding this dark one in history that we can work towards creating a more inclusive and compassionate future.

One of the poignant ways in which we remember the Holocaust is by honoring the lives saved by individuals such as Oskar Schindler. Schindler, a German industrialist, risked his own life and fortune to save over a thousand Jewish workers from the concentration camps. His story, immortalized in Steven Spielberg's film "Schindler's List," serves as a beacon of hope and redemption amidst the darkness of the Holocaust.

Honoring the lives saved by Schindler goes beyond simply acknowledging his heroic actions. It is a testament to the power of empathy and conscience in the face of unimaginable evil. Schindler's unwavering commitment to protecting the lives of his workers reminds us of the potential for individual acts of courage and resistance, even in the most dire circumstances.

Remembering and honoring the lives saved by Schindler also highlights the importance of recognizing the individual stories and experiences of those who survived the Holocaust. Each person who was saved by Schindler or other rescuers has a unique and valuable narrative that deserves to be heard and honored. Their stories offer us a window into the resilience and strength of the human spirit, and they remind us of the triumph of good in the face of overwhelming evil.

Beyond the moral imperative to remember and honor the lives saved by Schindler, there are practical reasons for doing so as well. By keeping the memory of the Holocaust alive, we are better equipped to educate future generations about the dangers of prejudice, intolerance, and unchecked power. The lessons of the Holocaust are timeless and universal, serving as reminders of the consequences of complacency, the power of collective action, and the importance of protecting human rights.

Remembering and honoring the lives saved by Schindler also serves as a reminder of the importance of individual responsibility in the face of injustice. Schindler's actions highlight the power of one person to make a difference, inspiring us all to consider how we can use our own positions of privilege and influence to advocate for those who are marginalized or oppressed. We are reminded that small acts of kindness and compassion can have a profound impact on the lives of others, just as Schindler's actions did. By keeping the memory of this dark one in history alive, we are reminded of the consequences of unchecked hatred and discrimination. Honoring the lives saved by individuals like Schindler serves as both a testament to the power of empathy and an inspiration for future generations to stand up against injustice. Through this collective remembrance, we can work towards a more inclusive and compassionate world, where the horrors of the past are never forgotten and never repeated.

Printed in Great Britain
by Amazon